NATHAN MAYNARD is a Trawlwoolway, pakana man and writer and director from Lutruwita/Tasmania. Nathan's first play, *The Season*, featured in the 2015 Yellamundie Festival (Moogahlin Arts). In 2016, Nathan finished a writer's attachment with Blue Rocket animation, where he helped produce and direct a palawa kani (a Tasmanian Aboriginal language) episode of the award-winning animation series *Little J & Big Cuz*. Nathan wrote an episode for the second series. In 2017 Nathan co-directed Jonathan Saunders' animation series *Zero Point*. Nathan collaborated with acclaimed Maori writer Jamie Mc Caskill on the children's play *Hide the Dog* (to be produced by Tasmania Performs). Nathan was co-creator, dramaturg and director of Naz Dickenson's debut play *CRUMBS* (2021 Yirramboi Festival, Melbourne). Nathan is currently working on the feature film project *Mosquito Jack* as a co-writer, alongside established writers Raimondo Cortese and Jonathan Auf Der Heide. Nathan was selected for the 2017 and 2019 PWA Aboriginal playwrights' retreat at Bundanon. He was also the recipient of the Tasmanian Aboriginal Artist of the Year Award in 2006 and 2013 and the recipient of the 2018 Tasmania Aboriginal of the Year Award. He received the 2018 Errol (Tasmanian Theatre Awards) for best writing and the 2018 Green Room Award for new writing for the Australian stage. Nathan was selected by the Australia Council as the Australian delegate to attend the 2018 Dublin Theatre Festival as part of the Next Stage Program.

L–R: Luke Carroll, Dom Mercer, Alex Malone and Nathan Maynard in rehearsal for Belvoir's production of AT WHAT COST? (Photo: Daniel Boud)

At What Cost?
Nathan Maynard

CURRENT THEATRE SERIES

First published in 2023
by Currency Press Pty Ltd,
Gadigal Land, Suite 310, 46-56 Kippax Street, Surry Hills NSW 2010, Australia
enquiries@currency.com.au
www.currency.com.au

in association with Belvoir

Copyright: *At What Cost?* © Nathan Maynard, 2023.

COPYING FOR EDUCATIONAL PURPOSES

The Australian *Copyright Act 1968* [Act] allows a maximum of one chapter or 10% of this book, whichever is the greater, to be copied by any educational institution for its educational purposes provided that that educational institution [or the body that administers it] has given a remuneration notice to Copyright Agency [CA] under the Act.

For details of the CA licence for educational institutions contact CA, 12/66 Goulburn Street, Sydney, NSW, 2000; tel: within Australia 1800 066 844 toll free; outside Australia 61 2 9394 7600; fax: 61 2 9394 7601; email: memberservices@copyright.com.au

COPYING FOR OTHER PURPOSES

Except as permitted under the Act, for example a fair dealing for the purposes of study, research, criticism or review, no part of this book may be reproduced, stored in a retrieval system, or transmitted in any form or by any means without prior written permission. All enquiries should be made to the publisher at the address above.

Any performance or public reading of *At What Cost?* is forbidden unless a licence has been received from the author or the author's agent. The purchase of this book in no way gives the purchaser the right to perform the play in public, whether by means of a staged production or a reading. All applications for public performance should be addressed to the author c/- Currency Press at the address above.

Typeset by Brighton Gray for Currency Press.
Cover image shows Luke Carroll; photo by Daniel Boud; cover design by Alphabet Studio.

Currency Press acknowledges the Traditional Owners of the Country on which we live and work. We pay our respects to all Aboriginal and Torres Strait Islander Elders, past and present.

 A catalogue record for this book is available from the National Library of Australia

Contents

Writer's note — vii

AT WHAT COST? — 1

L–R: Luke Carroll and Sandy Greenwood in rehearsal for Belvoir's production of AT WHAT COST? (Photo: Daniel Boud)

L–R: Abbie-Lee Lewis and Nathan Maynard in rehearsal for Belvoir's production of AT WHAT COST? (Photo: Daniel Boud)

Writer's note

Thank you, Belvoir!
You have my eternal gratitude for your commitment to getting this story on stages all around Australia.
Special thanks to Louise Gough, Dom Mercer, Eamon Flack, Aaron Beach, Sue Donnelly and Emily David.

I'd also like to thank:
Currency Press
For being brave and publishing this play.
Tasmania Performs
Their annual artist retreat is the place where I first pitched the idea of the play to other humans.
The Unconformity Festival
For giving me time and space to finish the play's first draft.
Moogahlin Performing Arts and the Yellamundie First Nations Playwriting Festival
For giving me the means to workshop and finish the play's second draft.
Playwriting Australia (now deceased)
For giving me time and space at their First Nations playwriting retreat, where I wrote the play's third draft.
Peter Matheson
Peter's not an organisation or a venue, but if he was, he'd be a library stacked with books about playwriting. Thank you for sharing this knowledge with me mate.
Rachael Maza
For supporting the work from its early days and for supporting me in my journey as a theatre maker.
Annette Downs
For being the best theatre mum a boy could have.
My Family
For putting up with me.
And last but not least:

The AT WHAT COST? *cast and crew*
You've helped me shape this story and its characters and the play is better for it.

The catch cry of the day is TRUTH TELLING.
The horror of this story is the Palawa people of Lutrawita's truth.

I dedicate this work to my sister *Sara Maynard*.
Who lives her life in the trenches fighting for our people.
We love you and appreciate your strength and dedication to our cause.

And my late cousin, *Elliot 'Bucky' Maynard*, whose celebrated work as an actor and theatre maker inspired me to use the craft of theatre to tell our people's stories.

Nayri nina-tu.
Thank you.

Nathan Maynard
April 2023

At What Cost? was first produced by Belvoir St Theatre at Belvoir, Gadigal country, Sydney, on 29 January 2022, with the following cast:

BOYD	Luke Carroll
NALA	Sandy Greenwood
GRACIE	Alex Malone
DANIEL	Ari Maza Long

Writer and Associate Director, Nathan Maynard
Director, Isaac Drandic
Set Designer, Jacob Nash
Costume Designer and Set Realiser, Keerthi Subramanyam
Lighting Designer, Chloe Ogilvie
Associate Lighting Designer, Kelsey Lee
Composer, Brendon Boney
Sound Designer, David Bergman
Dramaturgical Consultant, Peter Matheson
Intimacy and Fight Director, Nigel Poulton
Production Manager, Ren Kenward
Stage Manager, Natalie Moir
Assistant Stage Manager, Jen Jackson
Assistant Stage Manager, Brooke Kiss

L–R: Luke Carroll and Alex Malone in rehearsal for Belvoir's production of AT WHAT COST? (Photo: Daniel Boud)

L–R: Alex Malone and Sandy Greenwood in rehearsal for Belvoir's production of AT WHAT COST? (Photo: Daniel Boud)

CHARACTERS

BOYD MANSELL, 38, Putalina caretaker, Nala's husband.
NALA MANSELL, 32, Putalina caretaker, Boyd's wife.
DANIEL MANSELL, 30, Boyd's cousin.
GRACIE, 32, a camper.

SETTING

The story of *At What Cost?* takes place at the location known to the Tasmanian Aboriginal community as Putalina. Putalina is also known as Oyster Cove and it is located to the south of Hobart, Tasmania, Australia.

The set, which sits on top of a large visible shell midden, is divided into three sections: a hut, a tent, and a funeral pyre. The pyre grows through the play to a point where it reaches a significant height.

This play text went to press before the end of rehearsals and may differ from the play as performed.

*Luke Carroll in rehearsal for Belvoir's production of At What Cost?
(Photo: Daniel Boud)*

Complete darkness.

The sound of song in palawa language starts to trickle into the space.

The sounds of crying blend into the song.

As the song and wailing intensify the light of a funeral pyre (cremation fire) joins them in the space.

The fire and song continue to build in intensity. The sound of the fire joins in with the song and wailing, building and building until it reaches a peak which leaves no room for thought.

Snap.

SCENE ONE: RASPBERRIES

Putalina hut, afternoon. Day one.

The hut is basic, a double bed takes up half of it, the other half is filled with a wood heater, a table and a kitchen sink.

NALA MANSELL, BOYD's *pregnant wife, quietly enters during the following monologue.*

BOYD: We planted our black butts here and told the government we're claiming it back and there ain't nothing they can do about it.

When I say we, not me, I was only a five-month-old joey in Mum's belly.

Mum says I was created the first night the tents were put up. She reckons moinee, our people's creator spirit, was that happy we were back on this country he put me in her belly as a welcome home gift.

At same time as we were fighting for Putalina, we were also fighting a museum in England to get back the remains of one of our ancestors. Like we are now with William Lanne.

And like with Lanne, those white fellas weren't gunna part with that old fella. But we're fighters, us palawa, and we got him home. Back to his country.

And we held ceremony for that old fella, here at Putalina, and helped him home to the ancestors in the sky. Using fire and song.

But the government got wind of the ceremony and sent about twenty coppers down here, a tractor, a tractor driver and a monstrous rock in its bucket.

Their idea was to put that great big rock on top of the spot where we had cremated our ancestor. They wanted us gone from the property and they were sick of politely asking us to leave

BOYD *begins telling the following section of the story to* NALA *and her pregnant belly.*

Vroom vroom, the tractor goes.

And with the massive rock in its bucket, the tractor moves towards the ceremony site.

With locked arms we played the ultimate game of chicken and stood in the tractor's path.

Vroom vroom, the tractor built up speed.

But they underestimated our connection and respect for country, for our ancestor. Our passion for the cause. Our fight. We were gunna die if we had to. We locked our arms tighter.

It was the tractor who flinched first. Its driver, scared, put on the handbrake.

And then's the moment one of the elders began to sing.

NALA: Moinee ninghina mungalina.

BOYD: And we sang with them.

NALA / BOYD: Putalina palawa milyithina, Moinnee ningina mungalina.

BOYD: It rained that hard they say this place turned into a river before everyone's eyes.

And that tractor with the massive rock hanging from the front of it, it got bogged.

The more it went to move the tighter the country held on to it.

Our fellas sung louder.

NALA / BOYD: Moinee ninghina mungalina, putalina palawa milyithina.

BOYD: They dropped the rock and the country let go of its grip on the tractor. They drove away, never came back, and the rock it still sits where they dropped it today.

And us, in 1995 under the Aboriginal rights act, the gumberment officially gave us the land title to our country, to your country, Putalina.

NALA: Hey sexy.
BOYD: Yes sexy?
NALA: I have some news.

    Pause.

BOYD: You gunna tell me this news?
NALA: William Lanne is coming home.
BOYD: Noooo! Who told you this?
NALA: The Land Council rang me.
BOYD: Bullshit.
NALA: I wouldn't bullshit you about this, baby.
BOYD: He's coming home?
NALA: He's coming home.
NALA / BOYD: He's coming home!

    They swing each other around the open space in the hut. After a moment the reality of the news kicks in.

    BOYD, *sits down in shock.* NALA *sits down in front of him.*

BOYD: What about the poxy museum?
NALA: The world's changing and holding a hundred and fifty-year-old Aboriginal remains in your basement isn't exactly a good news story.
BOYD: When's he getting back?
NALA: Next week, Uncle Jimmy Everett and Sara Maynard are bringing him back to us.
BOYD: Poor bugger, imagine being stuck between that pair on a plane for thirty-odd hours.
NALA: I know, between Unc talking about his homemade Worcestershire sauce and Sara going on about her boys Bronson and Louis, if the old fella was alive, he wouldn't have got a word in anyways.

    They laugh.

    Beat.

There's more baby …
    The Land Council want *you* to make the fire.
    They want you to send him home. [*Pointing to the sky*] Up there.
Reunite him with the old fellas in the sky, like.

BOYD is overwhelmed and begins to cry, but he's trying to hide it.

BOYD: Me, the fire maker?

NALA: Yes you, you silly bugger.

They cuddle.

BOYD: What've I done to deserve the honour?

NALA: Boyd Mansell, my strong cultural man. You're the most respected man in our community.
You're our chief.

They kiss.

BOYD: I'm gunna have to start collecting wood, ay.

BOYD goes to run off and start collecting wood.

NALA: Wait, enjoy your wife for a bit first.

BOYD: All of her or just the big bits?

He goes to squeeze her breasts but NALA stops him.

NALA: Sorry babe, her big bits are sore.

BOYD: But they are so big!! The ancestors must be teasing me.

NALA: You can still kiss me.

They kiss and play around before BOYD stops.

BOYD: Did the Land Council say anything about that tent outside the gate?

NALA: They didn't know anything about it.
Probably just a lost tourist.

BOYD: As long as it's not a claimer.

NALA: Settle petal. Don't wreck the moment by talking 'bout them fellas.

BOYD: I'm lucky to have you Nala Mansell.

In play they accidentally knock NALA's belly. Cautious, they stop, and BOYD kisses NALA's belly.

NALA: Fucken oath, considering you have no dress sense.

BOYD: Righto.

NALA: And you have arse hairs like Bob Marley's dreads.

BOYD: Keep going.

NALA: And you couldn't find a G-spot with a set of clamps and a headtorch.

BOYD: I'm gunna tickle the shit out of you.

 BOYD *begins to playfully chase* NALA *around the table.*

NALA: No babe, please don't. I'll wet my pants.

BOYD: Are you trying to tempt me?

NALA: No don't. Swear on our unborn son that you won't tickle me.

BOYD: I swear.

NALA: Swear on our unborn son.

BOYD: I swear.

NALA: On our unborn son.

BOYD: [*muffling*] On our unborn son.

 BOYD *proceeds to blow raspberries on* NALA*'s belly.*

 DANIEL *enters, and waits down stage right.*

NALA: [*laughing*] Nooo! Boyd, no! You swore on your son.

BOYD: Technically raspberries and tickles are different.

 BOYD *continues to blow raspberries on her belly.*

NALA: [*laughing*] No they're not, they're just mouth tickles.

BOYD: I agree to disagree.

 BOYD *goes in for a big raspberry.*

 They continue to laugh.

 DANIEL *is sitting outside at the property's campfire. He yells out to* BOYD *inside the hut.*

DANIEL: What, are you standing me up cuz?

 BOYD *jumps up.*

BOYD: Crap, forgot all about Dan coming down!

NALA: I would've went shopping for baby clothes if I knew you two were having a playdate.

BOYD: Sorry babe, I forgot.

NALA: From now on every time you forget to tell me something, you have to go down on me.
 You'll either learn to how be a really good remember-er or learn how to be a really good licker-outer-er.

DANIEL: [*yelling*] Come on cuz.

BOYD: [*yelling*] Coming!

BOYD *grabs some beers, makes his way outside and meets his cousin* DANIEL *at Putalina's campfire.*

DANIEL: Too busy on the nest and forgot about your cousin didn't ya.

BOYD: Have a sook ya fucken sook.

Beat.

DANIEL: Mosquito dick.

BOYD: Raisin nuts.

DANIEL: Whatsup?

BOYD: Have you heard the news … Lanne's coming home.

DANIEL: Yeah brah, it's all over Facebook.

BOYD: Hope the community knew about it before it was plastered on that shit?
Who posted it. Wait, don't tell me. I betcha' it was Jill Mundy, the poxy Doris.

DANIEL: Maybe.
And I hear you're the fire maker brah.

BOYD: Muna.

DANIEL: Congrats cuz. Completely deserved.
But stuffed if I'd want that job. Too big of a responsibility to fuck up.

BOYD: Thanks for the reminder.

DANIEL: Got a beer?

BOYD: It's Cascade?

DANIEL: You need a loan or something?

BOYD: Nah, someone left a six-pack here and I'm not wasting my Boag's on you.

BOYD *hands* DANIEL *a beer.*

DANIEL: Do we know who belongs to the tent yet?

BOYD: Not yet.

DANIEL: [*drinking the beer*] Mutton bird island cold.

BOYD: How would you know what 'mutton bird island cold' is?
You've never been to a mutton bird island in your life.

DANIEL: You know the the Maynards invited me birding.

BOYD: There you go.

DANIEL: But I haven't got the leave from work up my sleeve.

BOYD: You're whipped as they come, ole man.
DANIEL: Whips and chains excite me.
BOYD: I bet they do, ya kinky devo.
DANIEL: Don't knock it until you try it baby.
BOYD: I'm busy trying to break free from those chains of colonisation, I don't need anymore.
DANIEL: You don't get sexual gratification from those?
BOYD: No. You do?
DANIEL: I can make anything work.
BOYD: You're seriously twisted!
DANIEL: I know.
BOYD: But do the women you chat to on Tinder know?
DANIEL: Fuck no. On there I'm a lovely bloke who dedicates his life to work for a non-profit organisation.
BOYD: I bet you forget to mention a non-profit organisation who directly compete with Aboriginal organisations for government Aboriginal allocated funds.
DANIEL: Here we go.
BOYD: And accept anyone who ticks the Aboriginal box on forms as mob.
DANIEL: Kiss me dick brah, you know I hate those tick-a-box cunts as much as you do.
BOYD: I'm only being a torment ole man.

Something in the distance gets DANIEL's *attention.*

DANIEL: Bro, someone just came out of the tent.

BOYD *has a look for himself.*

BOYD: Shit!
DANIEL: They're heading this way, fuck ya.
BOYD: Should I grab the gun?
DANIEL: What? No. We're not shooting them.
BOYD: Whatta we do then?
DANIEL: Say hello?

GRACIE, *a woman of a hippy appearance, approaches the campfire.*

GRACIE: Hi.

DANIEL / BOYD: Hello.

Pause

GRACIE: You wouldn't have a lighter I could buy?

BOYD: He's a dirty smoker.

GRACIE: [*to* DANIEL] It would save me driving in town to get one. Please!

DANIEL *hands* GRACIE *a lighter.*

DANIEL: It's temperamental.

GRACIE: The lighter or the owner?

DANIEL: The lighter, the owner has a beautiful temperament.

GRACIE *goes to hand the lighter back.*

I don't want your money.

BOYD: I'm Boyd and that dickhead is my cousin Daniel.

DANIEL: He loves me.

BOYD: Like a hole in the head.

DANIEL: And what's your name, tent mystery?

GRACIE *reaches out to shake hands.*

GRACIE: Gracie.

BOYD: Whatchya doing camping down here?

GRACIE: I'm actually doing research for my thesis.

DANIEL: What are you doing your faeces on … thesis.

BOYD: You idiot.

GRACIE: Dr William Crowther.

BOYD: Why in hell would you do a thesis on that man?

GRACIE: Because every time I see the statue of him in the city I want to punch something.

DANIEL: Sorry, who's this evil doctor guy?

BOYD: William Crowther, the anthropologist who cut into Lanne's dead body and sent his head to England.

GRACIE: In a jar of pickle.

BOYD: In a jar of pickle.

DANIEL: Oh, that evil doctor guy.

GRACIE: Tassie deserves to know the truth about the sadistic prick.

DANIEL: Did you know our community were just handed back Lanne's remains?

GRACIE: I heard that on the news. How good, I'm happy for you.
DANIEL / BOYD: Thanks.
> *Beat.*

GRACIE: You fellas the caretakers here?
DANIEL: He is. You and the sister girl been down here for how long?
BOYD: Fourteen months.
GRACIE: I'm envious. It's beautiful down here.
DANIEL: Why camp out there in the tea trees?
GRACIE: Because?
DANIEL: Watch out for the big snakes down that way.
GRACIE: You're having me on, I can tell by your eyes.
DANIEL: Fuck my honest sexy green eyes always giving me away.
GRACIE: They look more brown than green.
DANIEL: Anyways, don't camp out there, come and pitch your tent in here.
GRACIE: You sure?
DANIEL: Of course.
BOYD: Cuz, can we have a yarn?

> *They move away from* GRACIE *so they can speak in private.*

Whatta ya doing ole man, the gates to the property are shut to the public *remember*!
DANIEL: Cuz, she's not the public, she's one person.
BOYD: We're not allowed to let anyone in here without the Land Council's permission and they won't give it while we have that group of claimers from HAT trying to get in here. What if she's a HAT?
DANIEL: You're being paranoid and stupid.
BOYD: Ask her.
DANIEL: No.
BOYD: [*to* GRACIE] Are you from HAT?
GRACIE: Sorry?
BOYD: Are you part of that claiming group, Hidden Aboriginals of Tasmania.
GRACIE: No, I'm not part of any group sorry.
DANIEL: You right now ole man?
GRACIE: If it's any trouble, I can keep camping out there.

DANIEL: It's no trouble.
BOYD: Well—
DANIEL: [*to* BOYD, *under his breath*] Don't cockblock me.
BOYD: I'm gunna leave you to it. I'll catch ya later brus.

He nods to GRACIE.

DANIEL: Yeah see ya cuz.

DANIEL *grabs a beer from* BOYD*'s hand and gives it to* GRACIE.
BOYD *exits.*

SCENE TWO: TICK-A-BOXES

Continuing on from the last scene ...

GRACIE: Tell me about this place.
DANIEL: What do you know already miss student lady?
GRACIE: Nicknames aren't your specialty, are they?
DANIEL: Settle down.
GRACIE: What do I know ...
    I know it's called Oyster Cove and it's reoccupied Aboriginal land.
DANIEL: That's cheating, it says that on the sign coming in.
GRACIE: I know forty-seven palawa people were brought here from Wybelenna, Flinders Island in 1847 and that sadly most of them died here.
DANIEL: That's unfortunately true.
GRACIE: I know Lanne spent his last years here. And I know it's special. You can feel it when you walk around.
    It has an energy.
DANIEL: We call it Putalina.
GRACIE: Putalina.
DANIEL: They weren't gunna give it back to us.
GRACIE: Why on earth not?
DANIEL: Because they're the government.
GRACIE: Ha!
DANIEL: And now they've taken the property title away from the community and given it to the organisation Boyd was going on about. Hidden Aboriginals of Tasmania.
    And it's caused a massive shitstorm.

GRACIE: What's your community doing about it?
DANIEL: Same thing we did when we claimed this country back in the first place. We're planting our black butts here and we're not leaving.
GRACIE: Why don't the Land Council and this other group share the place?
DANIEL: You're funny. The Land Council and the mob don't accept them fellas as Aboriginal. They call them claimers. You know, white fellas who claim they're blackfella but they're not.
GRACIE: Why would you identify as Aboriginal if you weren't, I don't understand?
DANIEL: Me either.

Beat.

GRACIE: Pretty divisive of the government though.
DANIEL: Totally.

Beat

Anyways.
GRACIE: Anyways.

You don't want to give a girl a hand moving her tent? I can pay you a campfire dinner of tinned spaghetti on toast in return.
DANIEL: Deal. But do you mind if I grab my phone from the car first?

You see I work for a non-profit organisation looking after vulnerable people. And I'd hate it if I missed a call from someone that needed me.
GRACIE: You already have a dinner date with me, there's no need for the virtue signalling.
DANIEL: She's on to me.
GRACIE: Go get your phone.

DANIEL leaves.

GRACIE picks up some country and rolls it through her fingers and looks up at the sky.

GRACIE: Hello.

DANIEL returns and they leave for the tent.

SCENE THREE: GOOD NEWS FOR YOU SKY MOB

Cremation pyre.

BOYD *walks to a place on the property where there are three piles of rocks. He looks at the rocks and then looks at the sky for an extended silence before walking off stage.*

BOYD *walks back on stage with a pile of bush wood. Varying sizes of limb wood. He drops the wood near the piles of rocks. He walks off stage again before walking back on with another arm full of wood and dropping it next to the previous arm load. A pile has started to form. He looks at the pile and then looks up at the sky once again.*

BOYD: Ya you sky mob. I've come with good some news ... Lanne's coming home. Yep, he'll be back on our heart-shaped island next week. King Billy back on his home country.

Can you hear me truckanini, your king's coming home.

The mob have chosen me as the fire maker, and for me to get him up there to you, I'm gunna need you fellas to watch over the both of us, keep everything smooth, 'cause he deserves a smooth fast trip; you know with everything he's been through.

The savage bastards even removed his balls and sold his scrotum as a tobacco pouch.

What sicko fucks remove another man's dead balls.

Sorry for swearing you fellas.

But when I think of what that poor bugger went through it feels like my heart's going to fall out.

Please watch over us aye, you sky mob, and I'll do my bit from down here. I hope.

SCENE FOUR: THAT LAUGH

Putalina hut. Day seven.

NALA *is doing some weaving when* BOYD *walks in.*

NALA: Baby, you'll get him there.
BOYD: What if the fire doesn't burn hot enough, or it rains, or—

NALA: Stop stressing.

And anyway, first things first, they left Pommy land this morning which means we better get ready for the old fellas welcome home ceremony.

NALA puts her feet up on BOYD's *lap, and* BOYD *starts massaging.*

NALA: Shit that feels so good.
BOYD: You know my hands are magic, woman.
NALA: Get over yourself.

Babe, I've been thinking: What do you reckon about asking the Land Council for someone to replace you down here after bub's born?

BOYD: Nala, we've already spoke about this, I want my boy to be raised on country.
NALA: Hear me out. Not for good, just until he's not a tiny baby anymore. We could go and stay with Mum on Cape Barren. Mum would be such a help. And it would be nice for her to connect with her baby grandson.
BOYD: It's just too risky, babe. What if those HATs pricks walk themselves in.
NALA: I'm tired Boyd.
BOYD: [*raising his voice*] And you're not the only one Nala!

Silence.

Sorry babe. I didn't mean to yell at ya.

BOYD *kisses her.*

DANIEL *is heard laughing from outside.*

Is that Daniel's stupid flirting laugh I can hear?

BOYD *gets up and goes to the window.*

He's been down here every night this week.
NALA: Has he done his nuts over this woman?
BOYD: Must've.
NALA: I still haven't laid my eyes on her.
BOYD: He's heading over here.

Act normal like we didn't see anything.
NALA: I didn't.

BOYD: Then just act like you didn't. Quick.
NALA: Why?
BOYD: Act normal!

They scramble into stupid positions.

DANIEL walks into the hut and finds BOYD and NALA being all awkward.

DANIEL: Whattaya got to eat, I'm starving.

DANIEL starts looking through the cupboards.

What's up with you two?
NALA: Nothing.

Pause.

DANIEL: You pair of fuckers were watching me from the window, weren't you?
NALA: I wasn't.
BOYD: I was. I was watching your pathetic black crack try and flirt.
DANIEL: That wasn't flirting.
BOYD: Ole man, you were flicking hair you don't even have.
DANIEL: Fuck off!
BOYD: And that laugh.
DANIEL: What laugh.
NALA: [*imitating DANIEL's laugh*] Hahahahaha.
DANIEL: Maybe I was having a little crack.
BOYD: A little one?

BOYD and NALA imitate DANIEL's laugh.

DANIEL: She's a cool chick. I'm gunna take her over to Bruny Island for the day tomorrow.
NALA: Is this serious Daniel Mansell?

DANIEL shrugs his shoulders.

BOYD: Wish you asked me before you invited her in here.
DANIEL: [*laughing*] Sorry mister gatekeeper.
BOYD: It's all right for you, you just come and go.
DANIEL: [*laughing*] I'm planning on doing more coming than going.
NALA: Knock off tuck.
DANIEL: I'm gunna head home before the roos come out.

NALA: Gorn then.
BOYD: Take these weeriners with ya.

    BOYD *hands* DANIEL *a jar of* weeriners.

DANIEL: Legend brah.

    DANIEL *leaves.*

NALA: How does he do it?
BOYD: I can't know. He must be hung like a donkey.
NALA: It doesn't run in the family then.

    BOYD *playfully grabs* NALA *and kisses her neck, tickling her.*

    You wanna hear some serious news?
BOYD: Go.
NALA: I finished Lanne's basket.

    NALA *gets up from the table and grabs a traditional palawa woven basket and hands it to* BOYD.

BOYD: Baby, if my remains had to be held in something before I could be sent back to the ancestors, I wish It could be a basket of this craftsmanship. It's perfect.
NALA: You're just saying that because you have to.
BOYD: I'm saying it because it's a prime basket.

    NALA *is very happy with* BOYD*'s response.*

NALA: And I grabbed some peppermint gum to line it out with. Mould a nice soft cushion from it for his head to rest on.
    I mean 'him to rest on'. You know what I mean.
BOYD: I do.

SCENE FIVE: WEERINERS

Gracie's camp. Day eight.

Both GRACIE *and* DANIEL *walk into Gracie's camp.*

GRACIE: Thank you for a great day, Danny boy.
DANIEL: Have I earnt a kiss yet?
GRACIE: Calm your farm son. You wanna wine?
DANIEL: Wine not.
GRACIE: It's cheap shit. Remember I'm a student.

DANIEL: I wouldn't know the difference.
GRACIE: In that case it's a Penfolds Grange Sixty-One.
DANIEL: My favourite.
Wait, I nearly forgot. Shut your eyes.
GRACIE: Is this a trick to get a kiss out of me.
DANIEL: No, promise.
GRACIE: Okay, I'll trust you.

DANIEL *goes searching through and pulls out the jar of weerinerers that* BOYD *gave him and hands them to* GRACIE.

DANIEL: They taste better than they look.
GRACIE: Are these weerinerers?
DANIEL: Yep.
GRACIE: I've seen huge weerinerer middens along the coast here.
DANIEL: There you go.
Have you tried them before?
GRACIE: No, but I've always wanted to.
Where did you get them?
DANIEL: [*sheepishly*] Just around the point.
GRACIE: Can you please take me with you next time you go?
DANIEL: See if you like them first.
GRACIE: A palawa man culturally harvested them for me. I like them already.
DANIEL: [*gesturing for* GRACIE *to open her mouth*] Arhh.

DANIEL *feeds her one.*

And?
GRACIE: And I still like them. Thank you for sharing.
Close your eyes, I have something for you.

GRACIE *kisses* DANIEL.

DANIEL: See, was that so bad.
GRACIE: Give me another go and I'll be able to give you a more informed opinion.

They kiss again and cuddle up near the fire.

GRACIE: You're a nice surprise, Danny boy.
DANIEL: Ditto, tent mystery.
GRACIE: You can call me Gracie if you want.

DANIEL: Gracie tent mystery Quills.
GRACIE: Gracie Rose Quills.
DANIEL: A beautiful name for a beautiful woman.
GRACIE: Do you have a middle name?
DANIEL: Tim.
GRACIE: Daniel Tim Mansell.
   You know I used to hang around some Mansells back in my college days. We used to get smashed on boxy together in the city park.
DANIEL: I couldn't imagine you sitting in a park drinking box monster.
GRACIE: I was a naughty lost soul.
DANIEL: Boyd's partner Nala used to get around the park in the day.
GRACIE: Nala Everett?
DANIEL: Now Mansell, but yeah.
GRACIE: Is Nala here?
DANIEL: Yeah.
GRACIE: Bullshit!
DANIEL: No bullshit. C'mon, I'll take you over there.
GRACIE: Okay …

SCENE SIX: LEBANESE CUCUMBER

Putalina hut. Day eight, moments later.

NALA *and* BOYD *sit at the table.*

DANIEL *busts through the door.*

GRACIE: Nala Maynard!
NALA: Oh my fucken god, Grace Quills!
   Both women embrace each other with pure joy.
GRACIE: Look at you!
NALA: Nearly ready to pop.
GRACIE: You're glowing!
NALA: Bless.
   What are you doing here?
GRACIE: I'm camping here.
NALA: Fuck me, you're the Gracie in the tent.
GRACIE: That's me.

NALA: [*joking*] I wish I'd known earlier that the Gracie the boys were speaking of was you [*Pointing to* DANIEL] I would've told you to give this one here a wide birth.
GRACIE: Ha! I'm glad you didn't. I kinda like him.
DANIEL: Kinda, aye?

Beat.

GRACIE: That's a beautiful basket.
NALA: It has a very important job this basket.
GRACIE: Do you still string the shells?
NALA: Sure do, girl.
GRACIE: I remember that beautiful bracelet you used to wear back in the park.
DANIEL: Is that a Boag's I see there, brah?
BOYD: You're not bad, ya black bastard.

BOYD *hands* DANIEL *a beer.*

GRACIE: Sorry if we've crashed your night but when I found out Nala was Boyd's partner, I had to come say hi.
NALA: You're not crashing anything.
   You wanna cup of tea?
GRACIE: Yes please.
NALA: The last time I saw you girl, we were all in the park smashed off our heads
GRACIE: Like normal.
NALA: Like normal, and then you gifted Uncle Bob a little trinket of some sort and then took off.
GRACIE: It was my little going-away pressie to him.
NALA: You went away all right. You finished college and we didn't see you again. Where'd the hell you go?
GRACIE: Around Australia in a combi van.
NALA: [*laughing*] Fuck, we thought you were just going back to Bruny Island to give the liver a rest.
GRACIE: If I'm honest, I didn't know where I was going when I left Tassie. The old cliché, I was lost and didn't know who I was, blah blah. Enough about me, what have you been up to?
NALA: Nothing as interesting as you by the sounds of it.
BOYD: You met me.

NALA: I met shit lips there.
GRACIE: Did I meet you back in the day, Boyd?
NALA: Nah, he was living up north then.
BOYD: I can talk for myself Nala.
   I was living up north then.
NALA: That's where I met him. At the Lonnie NAIDOC ball, thinking he was all smooth because he just won the Aboriginal of the year award?
GRACIE: What did you win the award for?
DANIEL: For being a fuckin' legend.
BOYD: Long story.
NALA: He took the government to task on a road they were building through an important heritage site called Kutalina.
BOYD: Not that it made a difference.
NALA: It did to us.
GRACIE: A warrior.
NALA: Who never clocks out!
BOYD: Yeah yeah.
NALA: Tell us about your date, you fellas?
DANIEL: Tent mystery here let me parade her around Bruny Island like a tour guide and it turns out she was born and raised on the island.
NALA: You didn't tell him?
GRACIE: I may have forgot to mention it.
NALA: Classic. Hey, how's your mum?
GRACIE: Not with us anymore. The big C.
NALA: Ah mate, I'm sorry.
   She was a lovely lady, your mother.
GRACIE: She was an old grumpy arse.
NALA: [*laughing*] She was a strong bugger.
GRACIE: Strong alright. Lucky I came home when I did, she wasn't even going to tell me she was on her way out. Didn't want to bother anyone.
NALA: God bless her cotton socks.
   Now I feel like an idiot.
GRACIE: Don't be stupid, girl. You didn't know.
NALA: So what brought you back to Tassie then Gracie Quills?
GRACIE: My studies. The more I found out the more I realised I had to come back home and be closer to it.

NALA: The boys told me you're doing a PhD on Crowther. Exposing the sick cunt for what he was! Good on ya, girl.
GRACIE: Thank you.
BOYD: We have a mob-only thing we have to do tomorrow, Gracie. Do you mind not being here?
NALA: Oi, where's ya manners, brus?
GRACIE: It's okay, on Mondays the café at the library has a ten-dollar lunch special that's pretty good.
NALA: You couldn't do us a huge favour while you're in the city, girl, pick up our mail from the Land Council for us? It'd save me half a tank of fuel.
GRACIE: Of course.
NALA: Thanks, girl.
GRACIE: Is it still on Elizabeth Street?
BOYD: Yep, that place will never move.
GRACIE: Um, not meaning to be rude, but I think I should make the most of this moon and head down the beach for a walk.
DANIEL: I'll join you.
GRACIE: I was hoping you'd say that.
NALA: It was so good seeing you, Gracie.
GRACIE: And you too, girl.
NALA: Can we catch up later this week?
GRACIE: Please.
BOYD: [*to* DANIEL] Before you take off ole man, I need to yarn with ya.
DANIEL: [*to* GRACIE] I'll catch up.
NALA: I'll walk you out, girl.
GRACIE: Night Boyd.
BOYD: Night mate.

    GRACIE *leaves.*

The ole fella's remains will be here tomorrow. You gunna be here to help welcome him home?
DANIEL: Can't brus, I've gotta work. But I'll be here for his cremation ceremony on Sunday though.
BOYD: Priorities cuz.
DANIEL: Fuck brus, I have to work. I'll be here Sunday. Promise.
BOYD: Hurry up, your white woman is getting away.

DANIEL looks at BOYD confused.

DANIEL: You right cuz?

BOYD: Yeah, I'm right.

DANIEL leaves.

SCENE SEVEN: PULINGINA CEREMONY

Outside. Day nine.

A crowd wear kangaroo cloaks. During the ceremony that follows, BOYD is donned in a kangaroo skin by a community member. He is presented with a kelp bowl containing red ochre, which he uses to paint himself up. He is then handed William Lanne's remains in the basket NALA made.

The crowd sing the following song:

> ya pulingina milaythina nita.
> ya pulingina milaythina nita.
> mana milaythina, nina milaythina
> mana milaythina, nina milaythina
> ya pulingina milaythina nita.
> ya pulingina milaythina nita.
> mana milaythina, nina milaythina
> mana milaythina, nina milaythina
> Ki! Warr!

Lights up.

The crowd disperse.

BOYD is left with Lanne's remains in his arms.

NALA approaches and puts her hand on BOYD's shoulder.

NALA: In you we trust, Mansell.

NALA leaves.

BOYD: Ya uncle.

Mina, trawlwoolway man Boyd Mansell, Laura and Athol's grandson, Tasman's boy. Our fellas have chosen me to build you the sky ladder, and send you up to the sky mob.

And what an honour they have given me.

This is the spot where you're gunna leave from.

See those rocks there, that's where we've sent other old coes before you up to the sky mob. When you're gone, you'll have your own rocks to mark where you left from.

I've been collecting nothing but the best dry limbs for you aye, get that sky ladder as hot as we can get it and get you up there to them ancestors as fast as we can.

BOYD *puts Lanne down and starts building the pyre.*

After all these years, you're going home Unc. Up where there's wallaby bounding about everywhere, abalone under every swaying piece of bull kelp, biggest crayfish under every hanging rock ledge, where's there's mutton birds in every burrow.

Every night will be a full moon and you'll dance and sing with them ancestors until you see that morning star hit the dawn sky.

You'll be young and strong again, and your family will be there waiting for you. Your mum, your dad won't let go of you. They'll cuddle and kiss you and smell the top of your head like you're a boy again.

And everyone will be waiting to see you William Lanne.

When them ancestors see you coming, their black faces will light up like the Milky Way.

You're not even in the sky yet but everyone knows you're a star.

One day when I get up there, I'd be tickled pink if I could dance and hunt with you and if you could show me the old ways. For you to introduce me to my old fellas. The thought of meeting chief manalagenna.

I promise I'll get you there ole coe, I'll get you home to that sky mob, I swear on my unborn son's life I'll get you up to those ancestors.

And into your beautiful wife trukanini's waiting arms.

BOYD *continues to build the pyre.*

SCENE EIGHT: THANKS FOR GIVING US SPACE

Putalina hut. Day nine.

NALA's *at the table.* GRACIE *walks in and puts the mail on the table.*

NALA: You're a saviour, girl.

GRACIE: Boyd's right, nothing's changed in there.

NALA: Have you been in there before?

GRACIE: Yeah, remember Uncle Bob used to send us in there to grab his medication.

NALA: That's right.

GRACIE: You forgot to tell me about his passing. The lady at the desk had to tell me.

NALA: Oh shit, of course you wouldn't have known. Sorry girl.

GRACIE: He gave it a good nudge, I guess.

NALA: And some more. True to his word, he died with a flagon in his hand.

GRACIE: Do you remember when he'd look around the park and say—

NALA / GRACIE: [*imitating Uncle Bob*] 'I'm not poor my girl, look at me rich gardens.'

GRACIE: Christ I loved him. He knew who I was before I did.

NALA: I'd take you to his grave when we're in town next but—

NALA / GRACIE: [*imitating Uncle Bob*] 'Don't bother visiting me grave when I'm gone, 'cause I won't be there, I'll be hunting with them ancestors.'

GRACIE: I never noticed the massive portrait of William Lanne in there before, but it's stunning.

NALA: It's deadly, aye. I want a print of it for mine and Boyd's next house, if we ever get out of here.

GRACIE: Now that image should be turned into a statue and replace the filthy Crowther one.

NALA: True that.

    Beat.

GRACIE: Did you bring Lanne home today?

NALA: Yep, we sure did.

GRACIE: That makes me happy. Was it beautiful?
NALA: Very.
GRACIE: When are you guys having his cremation ceremony?
NALA: Sunday.
GRACIE: Do you reckon that maybe I could stay for it?
NALA: Ah, these things are normally a mob-only thing, girl.
GRACIE: And so they should be.
NALA: I got something for you but.
   I was going through some cupboards and found this.

   NALA *gets up and pulls out a mariner bracelet from a cupboard.*

GRACIE: Is this the bracelet from the park days?
NALA: Sure is.
GRACIE: No, I couldn't.
NALA: I insist. Uncle Bob would like you to have it too.
   They cuddle.

SCENE NINE: DREAM

Putalina hut. Night. Day ten.

BOYD *stands in his underwear, looking vaguely at the cremation spot.*

NALA: Babe, what are you doing out here?
BOYD: I seen his fire.
NALA: Whose?
BOYD: Uncle's. I saw his cremation. I saw his fire. But it wasn't us sitting around it. It was the claimers from HATs. They were sending him home.
NALA: Boyd, it was a dream.
BOYD: They were speaking our language, singing our songs, and dancing our dances.
NALA: C'mon babe, it's freezing.
BOYD: And Daniel was there with them.
NALA: It was a dream, Boyd.
BOYD: I could see it, I could hear it, I could feel it … the heat.
NALA: Baby, come back inside to bed.
   Beat.

BOYD: And you were there with them.

    NALA puts a blanket over BOYD*'s shoulders.*

NALA: C'mon, you'll catch yourself a cold.

    NALA takes BOYD *back inside.*

SCENE TEN: IS THIS A SAFE SPACE?

Gracie's camp. Day eleven.

GRACIE *is in her own world at her camp when* DANIEL *sneaks up and scares her.*

DANIEL: Boo!

GRACIE: You prick. Where have you been, I missed you.

DANIEL: I missed you too.
    I got held up at the Land Council talking to everyone.

    They kiss.

GRACIE: I was actually in the Land Council yesterday. I picked up Boyd and Nala's mail.

DANIEL: A couple fellas in there may have mentioned that.

GRACIE: What did they say?

DANIEL: That there was a hot white chick in there picking up mail for putalina. And asked if I was sleeping with her?

GRACIE: What did you say?

DANIEL: Not yet.

GRACIE: You're so fucken cheeky Daniel Mansell! If I didn't find it hot I'd knock that grin fair off your face.
    Why didn't I meet you back in the day?

DANIEL: I didn't grow up here.

GRACIE: Really!

DANIEL: Nah, I was born here but brought up in Melbourne.
    I've only been back for a couple of years.

GRACIE: Why'd you come home?

DANIEL: Because this is my country. It's hard to explain.

GRACIE: Nah, I get it. I do.
    The Land Council is such a great space.

DANIEL: It's not bad.

GRACIE: On my travels up the mainland, I met a heap of mob and got to hang out in a few Land Councils and Tassie's Land Council is just as good as any up there.

DANIEL: It's well run, I'll give them that.

GRACIE: They have a solid stance on Aboriginality though, don't they?

DANIEL: What do you mean?

GRACIE: Well you have to prove your connection in order to use their services right?

DANIEL: Yeah.

GRACIE: And listening to Boyd he has a cemented stance on Aboriginality too.

DANIEL: Most of the community do.

GRACIE: What's your view, are you like Land Council and Boyd hard ass or have you got your own view?

DANIEL: I have my own view.

GRACIE: And?

DANIEL: For fuck's sake don't tell Boyd I said this—

GRACIE: I won't.

DANIEL: I think if someone wants to claim they're palawa that's a good thing. It shows how far we've come since mob had to hide their identity.

GRACIE: I have a confession … Is this a safe space?

DANIEL: Of course.

GRACIE: When I was in the Land Council, I saw a pic of my grandfather in there …

DANIEL: What? Wait, who's your grandfather?

GRACIE: Well, my great-great-great-great-great-great-grandfather.

DANIEL: Who?

GRACIE: William Lanne.

Silence

DANIEL: Lanne?

GRACIE: Lanne.

DANIEL: Wow, why haven't you mentioned this earlier?

GRACIE: I didn't know you properly earlier. And with everything going on with palawa identity I was wary, extremely wary. The first night back in the state, I nearly had my lights punched out in a pub after revealing to a Cape Barren Islander I was a Lanne descendent.

I'm lucky she was kicked out before she could eloquently put it: 'Possum stop ya fucken teeth in, ya claiming dawg!'

DANIEL: I'm so sorry!

GRACIE: Thank you, but it wasn't your fault.

DANIEL: Are you actually down here researching Crowther?

GRACIE: Yes, but only because of his association with my grandfather Lanne. I'm doing my PhD on Grandfather.

I didn't mean to deceive you, but I was scared.

DANIEL: I get it, I do.

GRACIE: Thank you, Danny boy.

Can you tell please me everything you know about Grandfather's trip home. I'm busting to know.

DANIEL: If you give me a kiss afterwards.

GRACIE: You can have ten kisses afterwards.

DANIEL grabs GRACIE and puts her in his arms.

DANIEL: Well, the ole coe was picked up from the Royal College of Surgeons in England by two community delegates.

They washed him, cleansed him and then they gently wrapped him in kangaroo skins and flew him home to Hobart.

All teary-eyed we were there to meet him at the airport.

Then we brought him home, to putalina, where songs were sung for him, mob danced for him, and of course everyone cried for him some more … your grandfather, Lanne.

GRACIE: Tell me it was beautiful.

DANIEL: It was perfect.

GRACIE cries.

Mob decided he should have a week on country before he heads to the ancestors. So now he waits with Boyd and Nala until we send him up to the sky mob.

GRACIE: Oh babe, I wish I could be here for his cremation ceremony.

DANIEL: I don't think that'd be possible—

GRACIE: I know, Nala told me it's mob only.

DANIEL: Christ does Nala know that you're Lanne mob?

GRACIE: No, she hasn't got a clue.

DANIEL: Can we keep it that way, at least for now. If Boyd found out I'd be dead!

GRACIE: Found out that I'm a claimer?
   I don't want to claim anything, I just want to connect with other palawa people.
DANIEL: Gracie, I don't think like Boyd.
   They kiss.
   You know, I have never been with a palawa woman?
GRACIE: You must have.
DANIEL: I'm worried that I'm related to everyone.
GRACIE: Well aren't you lucky I'm Lanne mob and not a Bass Strait Islander.
DANIEL: Very lucky.
GRACIE: I have a crazy idea.
DANIEL: Do tell …
GRACIE: Let's go and have a look at the inside of my tent … Naked.
   They kiss and make their way to the tent.

SCENE ELEVEN: SIT ON THE GATE FOR ME BRAH

Cremation pyre. Morning. Day twelve.

BOYD *is in a daze.*

BOYD: Was it you who sent me those dreams Unc?
   DANIEL *enters.*
   During the following section, BOYD *slowly comes out of his agitated state but goes back into it by the end of the scene.*
DANIEL: Who you talking to?
BOYD: Just meself.
DANIEL: Righto.
BOYD: What you been doing? Don't answer that, I know what you been doing.
DANIEL: We've only been talking.
BOYD: Why's your fly undone then?
   DANIEL *panics and goes to do his fly up, but it isn't actually down.*
DANIEL: Smart cunt!
BOYD: Knock off with the swearing around Uncle here.
DANIEL: Oh shit, I didn't know the old fella was out here.

BOYD: I thought he'd wanna get out of the hut.
DANIEL: Fair enough.
BOYD: How's Gracie's studies going?
DANIEL: Yeah good.
BOYD: You fellas happy then?
DANIEL: It's only early days … but damn I've got the bug cuz.
BOYD: I can tell, your eyes are sparkling their tits off.
   She'll be pregnant soon and you'll be selling the Rexy and buying a minivan.
DANIEL: Doesn't matter what happens, I'll never be trading in the WRX.
BOYD: We'll see, we'll see. Help me with this piece will ya?

   BOYD *and* DANIEL *pick up a piece of wood and put it on the pyre.*

DANIEL: Here?
BOYD: Hang on city fella, you need air flow bro otherwise we'll smother the thing.
   Here, grab that and help me move it over here.
DANIEL: Cuz, don't laugh at me … but why are we cremating him?
BOYD: Why would I laugh?
DANIEL: Because I'm shame job.

   BOYD *grabs* DANIEL.

BOYD: Knock off, you may not have grown up here with ya mob, but you're our blood.

   Beat.

The spirits in the smoke, they carry the person's spirit up into the ancestor world.
DANIEL: That's extremely cool.
BOYD: And it's always been like that. You'll make my fire one day and them spirits will carry me up there.
DANIEL: You wanna lose some weight first.

   They laugh and carry on.

BOYD: For that, you can help me you little prick.
   Now a fire needs food, air and heat.
   The wood's the food. Gaps will give it air and the flame from the tussock grass I'll chuck in their later will give it the heat.
DANIEL: Did you do the fire for the last cremation here.

BOYD: I helped Uncle Jamie with it but this is my first in charge. That's why I wanted you to come and see me.

I was gunna see if you could be my man on the gate the day of the cremation. Make sure none of them claiming HAT group get in.

DANIEL: I don't think we have to worry about that.

BOYD: I don't wanna worry about it, that's why I'm asking you to be my gate bitch.

DANIEL: Okay.

BOYD: Legend, thank you.

DANIEL: All right, I gotta get going, aye.

BOYD: Too easy my brother. Wulika.

DANIEL begins to walk away.

Hey cuz, I love ya.

DANIEL: Yeah I know, like a hole in the head.

BOYD: Nah, like a brother.

DANIEL: Love ya too brah.

DANIEL leaves.

BOYD: Those tick-a-box scum won't get in here now, my uncle. Not now we've got some blood on the gate.

SCENE TWELVE: THE CRACKS

Continuing from the last scene.

BOYD *is outside dragging wood in the direction of the cremation fire.*

GRACIE *approaches.*

Lanne sits in his basket on a log of wood.

GRACIE: Hi Boyd.

BOYD: Gracie, how is ya?

GRACIE: I is well thank you. How could I not be on this beautiful bit of country. How do you put up with it?

BOYD: It's hard.

They laugh and then BOYD *gets back into prepping the fire.*

How's the research going?

GRACIE: Really good thank you.

BOYD: You probably won't be around for much longer then, aye?
GRACIE: I still have a few things I need to do.
BOYD: Can I help hurry it on for you?
GRACIE: Thanks but I know what I'm after.

GRACIE picks up a piece of wood with the intent to put on the pyre.

BOYD: Aye, aye, aye!! Leave that there!
GRACIE: Sorry, I was just helping.
BOYD: Look Gracie. I could get in big shit from my mob if they knew you were here.
　I'm gunna need you gone by Sunday morning.
GRACIE: Before Lanne's cremation ceremony?
BOYD: Yes. Before Lanne's cremation ceremony.

Pause.

GRACIE: How did your community end up with putalina?
　Correct me if I'm wrong, but your mob were traditionally from the north-east of the state.
BOYD: Yeah, trawlwoolway mob.
GRACIE: You're a long way from the trawlwoolway country here.
　How did a mob from north-east get the title to putalina?
BOYD: Due to a little thing called genocide, north-east palawa are the only mobs left.
GRACIE: Right …
BOYD: And under palawa lore that means we inherit putalina and the rest of the island.
GRACIE: Where do the members of the Hidden Aboriginals of Tasmania mob come from?
BOYD: Their diluted imaginations.
GRACIE: Do you accept anyone other than the families recognised by the Land Council?
BOYD: Why are you asking me this Gracie?
GRACIE: I heard that there are other palawa mobs, but your community don't recognise them?
BOYD: There's one Aboriginal community in Tassie and we're all from the north-east.
GRACIE: You don't think it's possible that some mob may have fallen through the cracks?

BOYD: Cracks, what cracks?
GRACIE: Maybe other mobs may have survived too?
From what I hear you wouldn't have declared your Aboriginality back in those times if you didn't have to.
From risk of persecution.
BOYD: We never denied who we are, buddy.
GRACIE: I didn't mean to upset you.
BOYD: You haven't upset me.
GRACIE: This Lanne's pyre?
BOYD: You really shouldn't be on this part of the property.

GRACIE *spots Lanne's basket and moves towards it.*

GRACIE: Is that Lanne in there?

BOYD *cuts her off before she gets there.*

BOYD: You need you leave.
GRACIE: Sorry, I'll go back to my tent, I should be studying anyway.
BOYD: Yeah.
GRACIE: Have a good arvo, Boyd.
BOYD: You too.
Remember you need to be gone by Sunday morning.

GRACIE *Leaves.* BOYD *is now suspect on* GRACIE *and watches her leave with suspicion in his eyes.*

SCENE THIRTEEN: COLES RUNNER

Putalina hut. Day twelve.

NALA *walks into the hut, puts a bag of groceries on the table and sits down.*

NALA: What a cunt of a day. First I had to go to the chemist and pick up a script, but they reckon no script was faxed through. So that took an hour of fuck arsing about before it was sorted! Then I went to Woollies and did the shopping before I realised I left the bank card here. So then I got Mum to send some money through to the post office for me to only go back to Woollies and find out they packed my full trolley of groceries back on the shelves. So out of protest I went to Coles, that was packed and then on the way here I got a flat fucken tyre which I had to change with tyre wrench that wouldn't look out of place on a play school set.

BOYD: I don't trust that Gracie.
NALA: [*sarcastically*] Oh, sorry Nala, that you've had such a shit day. But yes, Grace, what about her? Why are you suspect on her darl?
BOYD: Dunno, something's just not right about her.
NALA: What?
BOYD: Dunno.
   Do you think there's something suspect about her?
NALA: Like what?
BOYD: Dunno?
NALA: Use your words Boyd?
BOYD: Like why is she here? Like why would she need to camp down here to study Crowther? Wouldn't most of her work be done in the library? Okay, get a feel of the place, yeah, but she's been here for a week and a half now.
NALA: Maybe she loves it here? We love it here.
BOYD: But why do we love it here? If you had no connection to the place would you love it here?
NALA: It's pretty beautiful here babe.
BOYD: Baby, she owns land on Bruny Island. That place is fucken beautiful.
NALA: What are you saying babe?!
BOYD: What if she's a claimer and she's here for Lanne?
   NALA *sighs*.
   Earlier she was going on about other Aboriginal communities in Tassie falling through cracks and shit.
NALA: She probably heard stuff and wanted to ask someone in the know.
BOYD: Did she ever say anything about identifying when you used to get around with her?
NALA: No, and you're being a paranoid goose Mansell!
   Dan would have said something if she claimed she was mob.
BOYD: Maybe she hasn't said anything to the cuz.
NALA: Gracie's my mate, Boyd. Leave her alone. You're obsessed with these claimers.
BOYD: Obsessed, obsessed? These tick-a-box cunts are trying to steal our country from beneath our feet and I'm obsessed? Maybe you have your head in the sand?

NALA: Maybe I have my own opinion that differs from yours Boyd.
BOYD: What do you mean by that?
NALA: Nothing.
> I've had a cunt of a day and I just want a cup of tea.

NALA starts to make a cup of tea, there's a moment of silence.

BOYD: It's a good time to be a black fella if you're a claimer.
> The white fellas want our art, they want to hear our stories.
> There's more identified government jobs than there ever was.
> There's more blackfella scholarships than there ever was.
> But you know why this fucken gap isn't closing?
> 'Cause it's not us receiving these opportunities. It's the tick-a-boxers, they're cleaning up.
> Yes I'm obsessed … because I'm sick of being dispossessed.

BOYD walks over and picks up Lanne.

NALA: Baby, you have a massive job to do with the cremation, please focus your strong black energy on that. And forget about the claimers for a night.
BOYD: Fuck me Nala, did you just hear a word I said?
NALA: Yes I did Boyd. [*Yelling*] But I'm sick of hearing it. I need a rest, fuck ya!

BOYD walks out the door on a mission.

SCENE FOURTEN: I DON'T WANT TO BE FORCED TO PICK SIDES

Gracie's camp. Day twelve.

On a beautiful moonlit night, GRACIE *is venting to* DANIEL. *She is emotional and angry.*

GRACIE: He seriously believes that your mob were the only mob to survive the genocide. The fucken arrogance!
DANIEL: Don't take it personal baby.
GRACIE: How can I not take it personal? It's my identity. It's literally personal.

She takes a deep breath.

DANIEL: Did he ask why you were questioning him?

AT WHAT COST?

GRACIE: Maybe I should be straight out with him.
His problem is with people who say they're Aboriginal when they're not. I am, so the brother can't be angry with me.
DANIEL: Please don't speak to him now.
GRACIE: When should I speak to him then?
DANIEL: I don't know, not until after the cremation at least.
GRACIE: The cremation, the cremation of my ancestor. The cremation I'm not allowed to attend.
Because Boyd and the Land Council don't recognise anyone other than a few certain families.

GRACIE *begins to cry.*

I don't want to be in a place where I'm forced to pick sides.
DANIEL: Sides?
GRACIE: Land Council blacks and Hidden Aboriginals of Tasmania.
DANIEL: Baby, please don't say that. If Boyd heard you—
GRACIE: Boyd is part of the reason why people like me have to pick a side. At least HATs would recognise me as a palawa person. The other day when I was in town, I nearly called into their office to grab a membership.
DANIEL: Babe, you're angry but please don't talk like that.
GRACIE: It's easy for you Mansell, you have the name.
DANIEL: Did Boyd pick up on why you were questioning him?
GRACIE: You're safe Daniel, he doesn't know I'm a Lanne descendent. How would he know, your families were the only ones strong enough to survive, remember!
DANIEL: I don't wanna spend the night talking about this crap. Maybe I head home for the night and give you some space.

DANIEL *begins to leave.*

GRACIE: I'm sorry, please come back.
It fucken hurts when your own people don't see you.
DANIEL: I get it. But I can't handle talking about identity all the time. If it's not with Boyd, now it's with you.
GRACIE: Let's not talk about it then. I don't want you to go home. I'll be lonely without you.
DANIEL: I need you to promise you won't talk to Boyd though.
GRACIE: I promise. Can I have a cuddle?

DANIEL: You can have as many cuddles as you want.
GRACIE: It's a matter of how many I need.
DANIEL: You can have as many as you need, then.
GRACIE: I hope you think of me the same as I think of you?
DANIEL: Babe, I haven't thought of anyone the way I think of you.
GRACIE: Same.

SCENE FIFTEEN: HE WAS A WHALER

Gracie's camp. Day thirteen.

NALA: Hey.
GRACIE: Hey, you see that massive sea eagle earlier?
 Remember old Uncle Bob talking about how he reckoned he'd come back as a sea eagle next time. I couldn't help thinking maybe it was him.
NALA: He loved it down here. This is where he'd come to dry out.
GRACIE: Why not, it's a place for clarity.
NALA: Is that why you're here, clarity?
GRACIE: I'm here to study.
NALA: But does that have to be the only reason?

 Beat.

 Dan looks happy. It's nice.
GRACIE: I hope I have something to do with that.
NALA: I think you have a lot to do with that, girl.
 You know, since that fulla found his way back to community it hasn't always been easy for him, aye.
GRACIE: No?
NALA: No, it can be hard coming back to mob.
GRACIE: Even for a Mansell.
NALA: Even for a Mansell.
GRACIE: How do mob without a known name find their way back?
NALA: It's definitely harder for them mob.
GRACIE: I spoke to Boyd yesterday about the possibility of there being other mobs that aren't recognised by the Land Council, and he became quite agitated.
NALA: Boyd's under a lot of pressure at the moment.

GRACIE: Fair enough.
    Anyway—
NALA: He could learn how to ask questions before shutting the door on people though.
GRACIE: I worry because it wasn't too long ago that you fellas were fighting for the right to be recognised as palawa people. And it wouldn't be fair if the community are now denying others their connection.
NALA: I worry about that too. Shutting mob out without even asking the question.
GRACIE: Do you believe that sometimes people may not even know why they're connected to a place and they may have to figure it over time?
NALA: For sure girl.
GRACIE: I grew up in that bay, straight over there.
    Looking over the whitecap seas of the channel into this little bay. Wondering why I'm connected here.
NALA: And do you know why now?
GRACIE: I had a grandfather who was connected here.
NALA: That's pretty special.
GRACIE: I think so too.
NALA: Was he a soldier or a farmer, your grandfather?
GRACIE: A whaler.
NALA: A whaler.
    You know William Lanne was a whaler.
GRACIE: I do …
NALA: What was his name, your grandfather?
GRACIE: William Lanne.
NALA: I didn't know Lanne had children.
GRACIE: Think about it, sis.
    The government wanted everyone to think we were extinct.
    They told the world Lanne was the last full-blood palawa man, so they then can't come out and admit he had kids, can they?
NALA: You've got some timing on you, girl.
GRACIE: Please tell me Nala, when is the right time for someone like me to tell the community that they're palawa too? Because from my experience there's never a right time.

NALA: Why didn't you tell me back in our park days?
GRACIE: Because I didn't know then, girl. Mum kept it a secret from us because of risk of persecution.
    But then in her last week with us she was basically comatose.
    No acknowledgment of us being there, no movement, nothing. Until I whispered in her ear 'I know we're Lanne mob.'
    And suddenly her right eye started flickering. Winking at me. She held it in all those years and now all she could do was … wink at me with joy.

    Silence.

NALA: Girl, so I can get a better understanding, how does your family go back to Lanne?
GRACIE: We're not doing this, Nala.
NALA: Doing what?
GRACIE: An interrogation of my ancestry.
NALA: I'm only asking how your family are connected to Lanne.
GRACIE: Which sounds very much like an interrogation. I've been down this path before with other palawa mob and I know how it turns out.
NALA: How many years have you known me, girl?
GRACIE: I know Boyd's views in regards to palawa identity and I can only assume they're your views too.
NALA: Gracie, I'm not Boyd, I'm open to listening.
GRACIE: Thank you. But can we do this another time please? With what I've just disclosed and with what's going on. I'm feeling culturally unsafe.
NALA: Okay, but you let me know when you wanna have a yarn and share.
GRACIE: I will. Soon.
    Wulika.
NALA: Wulika.

    NALA *leaves.*

GRACIE: Hello Grandfather, I'm home.

SCENE SIXTEEN: YOU SAW IT TOO, AYE?

Cremation pyre. Day thirteen.

BOYD *is building the cremation pyre. He'd doing this with more intent than the last time we saw him building it.*

Lanne's basket sits at the botton of the pyre.

BOYD: She looked at you funny that Gracie did Unc. And then her eyes changed when she saw you. Did you notice? I did.
  I've got one eye open at all times. I've got one eye open at all times.

BOYD *leaves to get more wood.*

SCENE SEVENTEEN: WE NEED TO TELL HIM

Putalina hut. Day fourteen.

NALA *is at the table when* DANIEL *walks through the door.*

NALA: Sit.
DANIEL: Okay.

  DANIEL *takes a seat.*

NALA: Don't bullshit me now, do you know Gracie claims she's Lanne mob.
DANIEL: Yep …
NALA: Have you asked her how she is connected to Lanne?
DANIEL: No, why would I?
NALA: Don't you wanna know how?
DANIEL: I know she is and that's all that's important.
NALA: Has she offered an explanation to how?
DANIEL: No.
NALA: Then how do you know she is connected to Lanne?
DANIEL: Because she told me she's Lanne mob and that's good enough for me. Wait, how do you know she claims Lanne?
NALA: 'Cause I went and seen her yesterday and she told me.
DANIEL: Did you ask her how she's connected to Lanne?
NALA: She said was feeling threatened so we didn't end up going into it.
DANIEL: Sis, it's Gracie, you know her, she's not the claiming type.

NALA: I still can't validate her claims, can you?
DANIEL: C'mon, Gracie's right, it has to be possible for there to be mob out there we don't know about.
NALA: That doesn't mean Gracie is one of those mob.
DANIEL: But surely, we open our arms to these mob until we find out any different.
NALA: That's not how the community do things. We need to know how someone is mob, before we claim them as mob.
DANIEL: That thinking is back to front, I reckon.
NALA: She can't come to the cremation. Boyd would lose his shit.
DANIEL: Is it up to Boyd?
NALA: Daniel, the community would lose their shit. And yes, it is up to Boyd, he's the fire maker.
DANIEL: And the gatekeeper.
NALA: We have to tell him, you know.
DANIEL: Why?
NALA: Brah, if you want to keep your cousin and I wanna keep my man, we have to tell him, because god forbid he finds out some other way.

SCENE EIGHTEEN: HELLO GRANDFATHER

Cremation pyre. Day fourteen.

BOYD *is collecting wood for the pyre when* GRACIE *walks up to the bottom of the pyre and picks up the basket with Lanne inside.*

GRACIE: Hello Grandfather. I'm your granddaughter, Gracie. I'm glad you're home. We've missed you.
BOYD: [*yelling*] Gracie, put him down!
GRACIE: Hello Boyd.
BOYD: You have no right picking up that basket!!
GRACIE: Actually, I do.
   Brother, I need to talk to you.
   The man in this basket is my grandfather.
   I'm a William Lanne descendent.
BOYD: Hahaha. I fucken knew it.
   They told me I'm paranoid, but I knew it. I fucken knew it. I knew you were a tick-a-box.
GRACIE: Brother, I'm hoping we can have a yarn.

BOYD: Well, you're a fucken idiot then, ain't ya!
GRACIE: Brah, come on.
BOYD: Fuck off and get out of my face and get off this property.
GRACIE: Brother boy …
BOYD: Don't brother boy me, you gammin imposter dog!!
GRACIE: Wow, you are really angry.
BOYD: Get-the-fuck-off-my-land.
GRACIE: I'm not your enemy, brother boy. We're mob.
BOYD: We are not mob. You're an imposter dog.

He barks like a dog.

GRACIE: They want to divide and conquer. Don't let them.
BOYD: To divide suggests you're palawa and you're not palawa. So save me the bullshit!
GRACIE: Dan accepts me as palawa.
BOYD: Ha! As if!
GRACIE: He does.
BOYD: Dan doesn't know you're a claimer, and if he did, he would have kicked your tick-a-box arse out of here.
GRACIE: I think you'll find that he has an inclusive approach to people finding their way back to community.
And he's not the only one. Nala accepts me too.
BOYD: Bullshit.
GRACIE: Ask them.
BOYD: I will.
GRACIE: It's only you who has a problem with my identity, Boyd.
And maybe it's time for you to accept that things have changed.
BOYD: You're a lying piece of shit and you need to go now.
GRACIE: I'll be back for Grandfather's cremation ceremony.
BOYD: Over my dead body you'll be part of Uncle's ceremony!!
GRACIE: You haven't heard? The mob at HATs have applied for an injunction order for Grandfather's remains. I'll be at his ceremony, but will you?
BOYD: FUCK OFF NOW YOU TICK-A-BOX CUNT!

GRACIE leaves.

BOYD processes what's just happened for a moment and then picks up Lanne's basket and makes his way to the hut.

SCENE NINETEEN: STRATEGIC

Continuing from the last scene. Day fourteen.

NALA *is sitting in the hut when* BOYD *bursts through the door.*

BOYD: They're coming to take Uncle away.
    We're gunna lose him again Nala.
NALA: Who's coming to take him?
BOYD: HATS, fuck ya.
NALA: How do you know this?
BOYD: That tick-a-box Gracie told me.
    But you knew this, didn't you?
NALA: I know nothing about this Boyd.
BOYD: But you knew she was a claimer.
NALA: I only just found out.
BOYD: You accept her, don't you?
NALA: No babe, I don't.
BOYD: Are you lying?
NALA: No, I'm not lying, Boyd.

    BOYD *is manic, pacing around the hut.*

    Should we at least listen to her though … what if she is mob?

    BOYD *snaps.*

BOYD: [*yelling*] She's not our fucken mob!!
    Beat.
NALA: Okay babe, okay.
    Beat.
    But maybe we should be strategic and sit down with them?
BOYD: Who?
NALA: HATS.
BOYD: What …
NALA: Boyd, think about it, are you prepared to lose this place, to lose Lanne again? I'm not. I'd rather share his cremation with those fellas than not be part of it at all.
BOYD: Why are you saying this?

NALA: Because we have to be honest about the situation, babe.
As is the government legally own our identity, not us.
So, if the government accept them, we're gunna have to.
We have to play the game.
BOYD: You're one of them, aren't ya?
NALA: Don't be stupid.
BOYD: They've turned you!
NALA: No-one has turned me.
BOYD: Liar!
NALA: I'm being strategic!
BOYD: No, they've turned you, they've turned Daniel.
I saw it in my dream ... you sit around Uncle's fire with them.
And they know our dances and songs, 'cause you teach them ...
NALA: Boyd, you're not thinking straight.
BOYD: No, no, no, you're both traitors, traitors to our people, traitors to our ancestors. Fucken shame jobs the pair of ya!

BOYD *runs out of the hut.*

SCENE TWENTY: YOU'RE NOT THE GATEKEEPER

Cremation pyre. Day fourteen.

BOYD *is sitting on top of the pyre. Lanne's skull is sitting up there with him.* DANIEL *walks up.*

BOYD: Come on you dogs, I dare you to try and fucken come in here and take him. Bring your big fucken tractor back, I don't give a fuck you imposter cunts! You try and take my ancestor I'll run through every fucken one of ya!

BOYD *hears a noise which grabs his attention.*

DANIEL: Brus, whatta you doing?
BOYD: If it's not the validation prince himself!
You think you and your mates are gunna come and take Lanne, aye!
DANIEL: What are you talking about brah?
BOYD: Ha! But I've seen it. You're with them when they cremate him.
I SAW YOU WITH THEM!
DANIEL: You're not well, cuz.
BOYD: Your woman turned you into a sell-out.

DANIEL: Brah, she's done nothing.

BOYD: Like fuck the dog hasn't!

DANIEL: Brother, remember when I first came back into the community and it took a while for the community to accept me.

BOYD: Not the same. Not even close. [*Yelling*] We know who you belong to!

DANIEL: Did you even ask her about her connection to Lanne?

BOYD: Maybe you can fill me in brah?

Silence.

You haven't asked her, have you?

Sold out for a new shiny 'tick-a-box' box, didn't ya? And now ya passing on your sexually transmitted cultural knowledge.

DANIEL: Get fucked. I'm allowed to have my own opinion about our identity!

BOYD: You've picked your side and now you belong on that side of the gate. You're a fucken shame job.

DANIEL: Get fucked cunt.

You might be the gatekeeper to putalina but you're not the gatekeeper to our community.

BOYD: No, I'm not, and neither are you … our bloodline is our gatekeeper. The ancestors will spit on you.

[*Speaking to the sky mob*] Hey sky mob, spit on him, spit on the sell-out dog I used to call my cousin.

BOYD *spits in* DANIEL*'s face.*

DANIEL *punches* BOYD *and knocks him out.*

DANIEL *goes, leaving* BOYD *unconscious on the ground.*

SCENE TWENTY ONE: WHY WOULD I LEAVE?

Gracie's camp. Day fourteen.

NALA *visits Gracie's camp.*

NALA: I'm gunna need you to leave.

GRACIE: Ah sis, I was genuinely hoping that the palawa communities of lutruwita could live united.

NALA: Community, not 'communities'.

GRACIE: I understand, you're under pressure from Boyd.

NALA: Gracie, leave.
GRACIE: Ha! Maybe it's you who should leave Nala.
  It's our land and we'll take it back … like we're taking Grandfather back.
NALA: You're gunna get sick, you know. The spirits will punish you.
GRACIE: You fullas are not even Lanne mob.
NALA: Please tell us how you go back to Lanne, Gracie?
GRACIE: Do you want me to pull out my family tree? I carry it around with me for moments like this, never know when you're gunna be stopped by the Aboriginal gestapo: Here miss, here's my papers miss. Please don't beat me miss.
  He's one of my grandfathers Nala, you know this already.
NALA: But how do you go back to him?
GRACIE: I don't feel culturally safe answering that question today.
NALA: Cut the bullshit Gracie.
GRACIE: I don't have to tell you.

   NALA *grabs* GRACIE

NALA: You claim me, you claim us! We have a right to know how!
GRACIE: I'm not claiming you, I'm claiming Lanne.
NALA: But that's where you're wrong.
  We're connected through our land, through our language, through our stories, through our history. I'm one thread of a map made of palawa DNA, of palawa linage, of palawa bloodline. I'm one part of the palawa family, like Lanne. How are you our family, Gracie?
GRACIE: You lot need paper trails.
NALA: Lies! We don't need a paper trail but we need a bloodline.
GRACIE: Not everything was recorded.
  Our old fellas know the bloodline, my mother knew the bloodline. And that's all that should matter.
NALA: And she's not with us anymore, so we can't ask her. Right?
GRACIE: And what about Uncle Bob Everett. How many times did he say 'you're mob girl, I can see it in your face'?
NALA: He said that to anyone who needed to belong.
  William Lanne isn't your grandfather, Gracie.
  You heard of Betsy Clarke? One of the last black women to be here with Lanne before his death.

Betsy Clarke quote: 'William Lanne. He sad man. Because he can't have no children.'

Beat.

You have no blood connection to Lanne, Gracie, it's impossible.
GRACIE: I have a connection!
NALA: How, Gracie?
GRACIE: Does it matter if I don't know how ... or know where it is? I can feel my connection and that's all that should matter!!
Can't I just feel it, can't I just know within my spirit? Why isn't that enough? Can't I belong to something special too?
NALA: Yes you can Gracie, but that something special isn't us. You need a blood connection to belong to us.
GRACIE: [*pulling herself together*] I don't have to prove myself to any of you.
NALA: No, Gracie, not anymore you don't. Now you only have to tick a box on a government form.

DANIEL enters. He's distraught about the fight with BOYD. He's crying.

DANIEL: I hit him, I fucken hit him.
NALA: Who?
DANIEL: Boyd. He came at me first.
NALA: Where is he?
DANIEL: The pyre.

NALA leaves.

Maybe you should go home until things cool down.
GRACIE: I'm not going anywhere.
DANIEL: Babe, there's too much tension, it'll be better for everyone if you go.
GRACIE: Daniel, I'm finally on country. On Aboriginal land. My land. Why would I jeopardise that and leave? I'll never be allowed back in if I leave.
DANIEL: Babe, please.
GRACIE: I'm not leaving.

Beat.

DANIEL: Gracie ... how do you go back to Lanne?

SCENE TWENTY TWO: WHERE WERE THEY?

Cremation pyre. Day fourteen.
BOYD *wakes up from being knocked out.*

BOYD: These claimers are not part of this country's story.
They're not part of our story. They're not part of my story.
Beat. He shifts.
Where were they when I used to get called Abo at school?
Or when the teachers used to tell me I'm a half-caste.
Where were they when the cops used to bash me 'cause I'm 'Mansell scum'?
And where they when my nan used to break down talking about her dead sons who died locked up?
Tell me where they were when my uncle Colin was dragged out of bed, only to be found hours later swinging in his cell by his black neck.
And please tell me where they were after my sixteen-year-old cousin Lou Lou walked into the Launceston Trades Hotel, pulled a sawn-off shotgun out of her backpack, and blew her head off. Because the family sure coulda needed them then.
Where the fuck were they then, aye?
Had some book not told them they were black yet?
Had they not felt a connection yet?
Had the government not told them they were palawa yet?
[*Sadly*] And now my mob sit with them around our fire.
BOYD *see's Lanne spirit and kneels down before him.*
Uncle, is that you?
You need to go now don't you. Before you're lost for good.
Before your spirit is lost for good. Because those thieves have made their way into your story, old coe. And people who can't listen when they're told let them in. [*Yelling*] And they had no right! They had no right!
You look tired. You can't fight no more. You can't suffer it no longer, can ya ...

You've fought from the day the creator spirit put you in your mother's belly, but that tractor never stopped coming and it never will. It never will.

Future NALA *enters with a baby in her arms.*

BOYD *picks up a traditional fire torch and lights it.*

But it's gunna be all good now Unc.

We're gunna go where there's wallaby bounding everywhere.

Where there's an abalone under every swaying piece of bull kelp.

Where there's crayfish under every hanging rock ledge.

Where there's a mutton bird in every burrow.

Beat.

We're gunna go where our people are happy.

BOYD *ignites the pyre with the fire torch.*

EPILOGUE

Complete darkness.

The sound of song in language starts to trickle into the space.

The sounds of crying blend into the song.

As the song and wailing intensify, the light of a funeral pyre (cremation fire) joins them in the space.

The fire and song continue to build in intensity. The sound of the fire joins the song and wailing. Building and building until it reaches a peak which leaves no room for thought.

Snap.

Lights down, darkness.

THE END